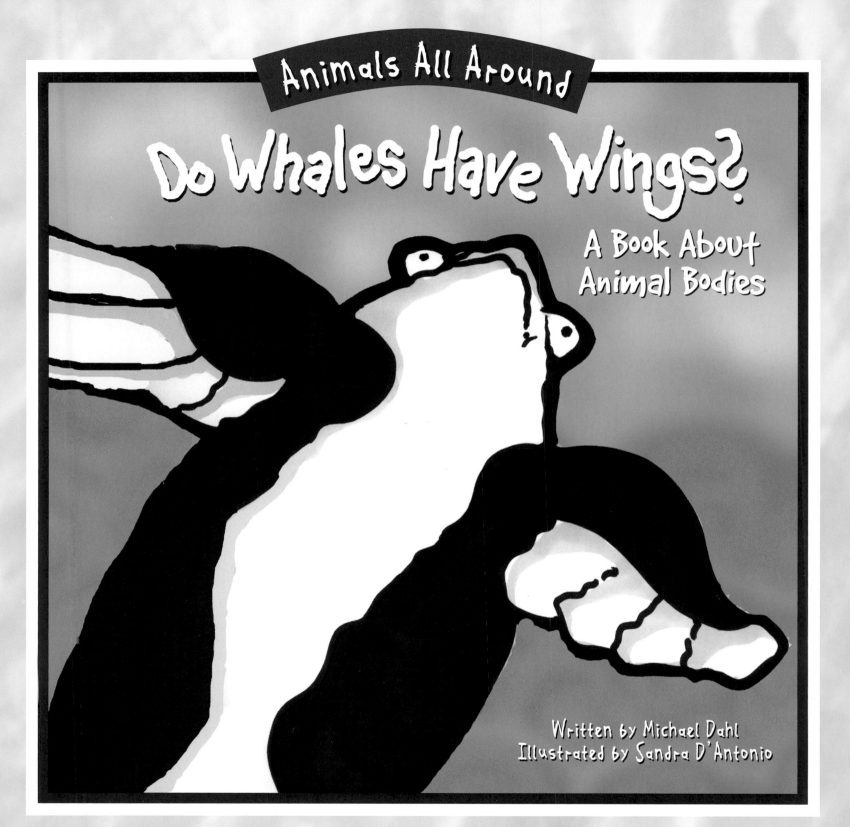

Animals All Around

Do Whales Have Wings?

A Book About Animal Bodies

Written by Michael Dahl

Illustrated by Sandra D'Antonio

Content Consultant: Kathleen E. Hunt, Ph.D.
Research Scientist and Lecturer, Zoology Department
University of Washington, Seattle, Washington

Reading Consultant: Susan Kesselring, M.A., Literacy Educator
Rosemount-Apple Valley-Eagan (Minnesota) School District

PICTURE WINDOW BOOKS

MINNEAPOLIS, MINNESOTA

Animals All Around series editor: Peggy Henrikson
Page production: The Design Lab
The illustrations in this book were rendered in marker.

Picture Window Books
5115 Excelsior Boulevard
Suite 232
Minneapolis, MN 55416
1-877-845-8392
www.picturewindowbooks.com

Printed in the United States of America.
1 2 3 4 5 6 08 07 06 05 04 03

Library of Congress Cataloging-in-Publication Data
Dahl, Michael.
Do whales have wings? / written by Michael Dahl ; illustrated by
Sandra D'Antonio.
p. cm. — (Animals all around)
Summary: Introduces varying parts of the anatomy of a number
of different animals.
ISBN 1-4048-0103-0 (lib. bdg.)
1. Anatomy—Juvenile literature. [1. Anatomy.] I. D'Antonio,
Sandra, 1956— ill. II. Title.
QL806.5 .D25 2003
573.7'9—dc21
2002155019

Do Whales Have Wings?

No! Butterflies have wings.

Monarch butterflies have four strong wings that flutter and flap. Thick, black veins keep their orange wings stiff. These butterflies fly over one thousand miles to be in a warm place for the winter.

Do whales have beaks ?

No! Parrots have beaks.

Parrots have sharp, curving beaks. Their powerful beaks can break open the hard shells of seeds and nuts for the parrots to eat. Parrots' beaks can be very colorful. Sometimes they are bright red or flaming orange.

Do whales have feathers?

No!
Owls have
feathers.

Owls have soft, fluffy feathers. Special feathers soften the swooping sound of the owl's wide wings. Hunting owls can silently and quickly fly through the forest and sneak up on their prey.

Do whales have legs ?

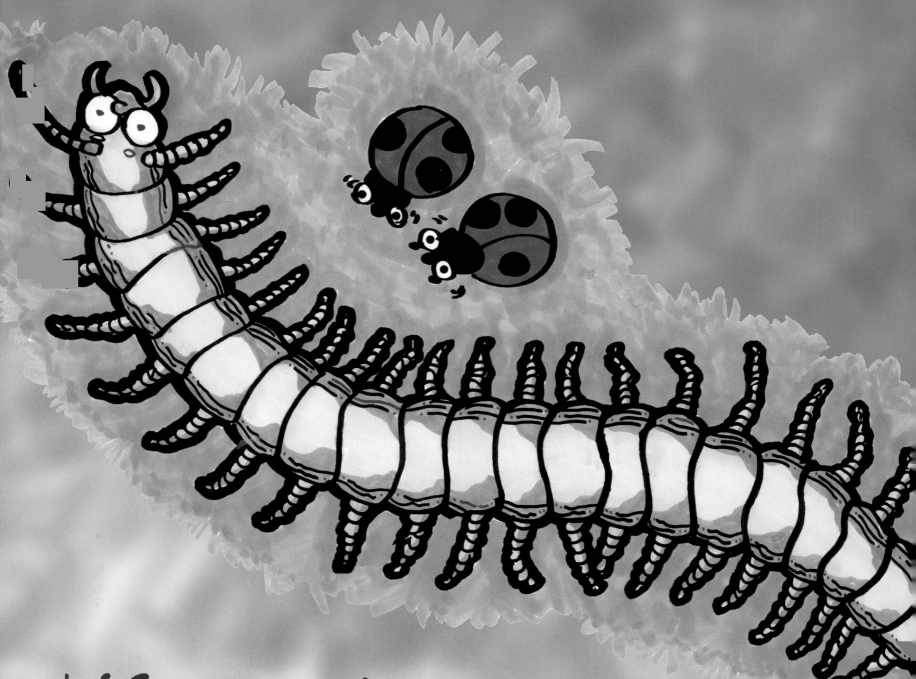

No! Centipedes have legs.

Centipedes crawl quickly, searching for food at night. A centipede's body is divided into parts, like a roll of coins. Each part has a pair of long, skinny legs. Grown-up centipedes can have as many as 177 pairs of legs.

10

Do whales have tusks ?

No! Walruses have tusks.

A heavy walrus glides gracefully underwater. But it isn't so easy for the walrus to climb out. The walrus uses its long, sharp tusks to pull its big body up onto an ice floe or a rocky shore.

Do whales have paws ?

No! Puppies have paws.

Tiny puppies with big, padded paws often grow into very large dogs. Dogs that pull sleds in the snow of the north have very furry paws. These sled dogs often wear soft booties to protect their paws from ice and snow.

Do whales have claws?

No! Lobsters have claws.

Lobsters crawl on the floor of the ocean, waving their heavy claws. One claw is strong enough to crush a crab shell. The other claw has sharp teeth that can rip out the crabmeat for a tasty meal.

Do whales have horns ?

No! Bulls have horns.

Bulls grow hard, heavy horns on the tops of their heads. A bull's horns are longer and sharper than a cow's horns. As the bull grows bigger, his horns curve and spread wider from tip to tip.

Do whales have hooves?

No! Mountain goats have hooves.

Mountain goats can climb up steep, rocky ledges. Thick, rubbery pads on the goats' hooves act like suction cups. The pads help the hooves cling tightly to the rock.

Do whales have fins ?

Yes! Whales have fins.

Whales have fins and flippers
and flukes on their tails
for flapping and flashing
and swishing and splashing
long bubbly trails.

Animal Bodies

Some animals have bright, colorful bodies.

brilliant wings	monarch butterflies
flashing beaks	parrots

Some animals have bodies that blend with their surroundings.

dark as deep water	walruses
white as snow	mountain goats

Some animals have hard bodies.

thick shells	lobsters
crunchy skin	centipedes

Some animals have soft bodies.

smooth, hairy hide	bulls
fuzzy fur	puppies
fluffy feathers	owls

Some animals' bodies are too big to hide!

heavy hulks	whales

Words to Know

beak—the hard, front part of a bird's mouth

fin—a flap sticking out from the back of the bodies of some whales. Whales use their fins for moving steadily through the water.

flipper—a wide, flat flap sticking out from the side of a whale's body that it uses for swimming and steering

fluke—the wide, flat end of a whale's tail

prey—an animal that is hunted by another animal for food

tusk—one of two, very long, pointed teeth that curve out of the mouths of some animals such as the walrus

suction cup—a thin, rubbery cup that sticks to things

veins—small, stiff, tubes that help a butterfly wing keep its shape

whale—a large animal that lives in the ocean. A whale looks like a fish but is actually a mammal that breathes air.

Index

To Learn More

At the Library

Brown, Marc. *Wings on Things*. New York: Beginner Books, 1982.

Kee, Lisa Morris. *Whose Mouth Is This? A Look at Bills, Suckers, and Tubes*. Minneapolis: Picture Window Books, 2003.

Miles, Elizabeth. *Legs and Feet*. Chicago: Heinemann Library, 2003.

Moses, Brian. *Munching, Crunching, Sniffing and Snooping*. New York: DK Pub., 1999.

On the Web

Minnesota Zoo
http://www.mnzoo.com/index.asp
Explore the Minnesota Zoo online, including a Family Farm. See pictures of the animals and visit the Kids' Corner with animal puzzles, games, and coloring sheets.

Zoological Society of San Diego: e-zoo
http://www.sandiegozoo.org/virtualzoo/homepage.html
Visit this virtual zoo with a Kid Territory. The section for kids includes animal profiles, games, zoo crafts, and even animal-theme recipes, such as Warthog Waffles.

Want to learn more about animal bodies?
Visit FACT HOUND at http://www.facthound.com.